Copyright © 2024 Antionette Barnes All rights reserved

The characters and events portrayed in this book are fictitious.
Any similarity to real persons, living or dead,
is coincidental and not intended by the author.

No part of this book may be reproduced, or stored in
a retrieval system, or transmitted in any form, or
by any means, electronic, mechanical, photocopying, recording,
or otherwise, without express written permission of the publisher.

ISBN: 978-1-7370589-4-6

Printed in the United States of America

THE POET IN YOU, THE POET IN ME, THE POET IN US

By: Antionette Barnes

AT THIS POINT

At this point in my life,
I am in my gratitude phase
Because at this point
I am moving differently

At this point,
I am moving forward
Releasing what I need to release
Along the way

At this point,
I have developed a new love for myself
Treating myself with the upmost respect
Maturity at its finest

The poet in you,

        the poet in me,

                the poet in us

A. Barnes

Contents:

1. Be specific with me
2. Somehow
3. You left
4. Away from you
5. Deserve to be happy
6. Moving on
7. Submissive
8. Inspirations from you
9. Where do I start?
10. Closure
11. Letting go
12. En route
13. Think back
14. Fading away
15. Just for the record
16. Free time
17. I'm
18. Expect
19. Before
20. Sometimes
21. Someone
22. Whole day
23. Proper care
24. Introducing
25. Moments

Be specific with me

You have to be specific with me

You

Yeah, you

Are else

If you don't

I will get to assuming

I don't like to assume

So, be specific with me

Before assumptions starts

And I start jumping to conclusions

Be specific with me

Don't beat around the bush

Antionette Barnes

"Before assumptions starts"

—Poetic Tamara

Somehow

As days go on,
I think about you more and more
But I only think about you
Whenever I'm not busy

Somehow, I wish that you know that I am thinking of you
You're in my thoughts
When you shouldn't be
Because you're there rent free

If there was a way somehow,
For the message to get to you
That I miss you
It would make me smile even bigger

I wish you know somehow,
That I wish you the best in life
I have to keep my distant
And I want you to know that I'm doing this for the better

"That I wish you the best in life"

—Poetic Tamara

3 You left

You're going to hate that you left
Going to be all up in your feelings
When you see me elevate
When you see me move on

Don't be trying to get me back
You shouldn't have left here in the first place
You decided to leave
You left

You left me alone with my feelings
With our memories
You left
Watch me move on

You're going to hate it when I get over you
You left me
With no choice
I have to do what's best for me

"You left me alone with my feelings"

–Poetic Tamara

Away from you

I just had to get away from you

I found myself always wanting to be under you

Not wanting to do nothing

Not wanting to go nowhere

Being lazy

I hate to be lazy

Getting away from you

Was heavy on my mind

My energy was being drained

Give me my time back

I wasted too much time on you

I got away from you

It was past time for me to get away

I had to get my energy back

Regain my focus

Too much time was wasted on you

"Too much time was wasted on you"

—Poetic Tamara

Deserve to be happy 5

You told me that you don't do relationships
That you love your peace
Next thing I know,
You popped up in a relationship

I started looking at myself
Trying to see what do she have
That I don't
I deserve to be happy

Yet, I started focusing too much on her
I wanted you
I started changing my ways
For you

You didn't notice
You cut me off
That's what made me regain my focus on me
I deserve to be happy

"That's what made me regain my focus on me"

−Poetic Tamara

Moving on (6)

I'm a dangerous woman right now

I've learned to move on

I've learned to do me

I'm moving on

I have no desire to stay where I'm at

There is no time to focus on the past

I'm not my past

I'm moving on

Focusing on my future

Focusing on myself

Not dwelling on what might have been

I'm moving on

"I have no desire to stay where I'm at"

-Poetic Tamara

Submissive

You used to always try to tell me what to do
When you wasn't what it do
How do you expect me to look towards you for leadership?
I didn't see myself submitting to you

I'm not the submissive type
But for the right one
I might be
Take some loads off of me

I will not submit to the wrong person
I rather be alone
Doing my own thing
Before I be submissive

To a person not worth submitting to
How does an independent woman supposed to be submissive?
Answer me that?
Yeah, yeah, I'm good

"How does an independent woman supposed to be submissive?"

−Poetic Tamara

THE POET IN YOU, THE POET IN ME, THE POET IN US

"I will not submit to the wrong person
I rather be alone
Doing my own thing
Before I be submissive"

Sub | missive

Inspirations from you (8)

I used to listen to you a lot

I mean really listen to you

I inner stood where you were coming from

For the most part

I be like "Man, yeah. I feel you."

I love the way you speak facts

You used to always speak your truth

You were such an inspiration to me

I used to get a lot of inspirations from you

You be knowing what you be talking about

I learned a lot from you over the course of time

Sad to say that we drifted apart

Somehow, we need to get back cool

Come back together

So, I can hear your truths

I had got a lot of inspirations from you

> "I love the way you speak facts"
>
> —Poetic Tamara

Where do I start?

Where do I start?

I'm trying to figure that out

Where do I start?

What can I say?

I stay out of people faces

I know how to

Stay in my lane

In my own world

Where do I start?

The best version of me

Is coming about

The old me is dying

The new me is taking over

Where do I start?

A fresh start

A better way of thinking

> "THE NEW ME IS TAKING OVER"
>
> –Poetic Tamara

10 Closure

I used to always think "Why me?"
Why do I always get hurt
By the ones that I love the most?
I used to always seek closure

I needed this pain to leave
So, I needed to know why
I really needed some closure
Take this pain away

Tell me why you left
I used to think of ways
Things could be different
Then maybe I wouldn't have felt

The pain that I had felt
I was hurting so much
My mind kept wondering
I needed my closure

"I used to always seek closure"
—Poetic Tamara

THE POET IN YOU, THE POET IN ME, THE POET IN US

"I needed this pain to leave
So, I needed to know why
I really needed some closure
Take this pain away"

Clo | sure

Letting go

Letting go

Man, that was a tough thing that I had to do

But I had to do what was best for me

You acted like you loved me

Love from you didn't really show

At least not no real love

I got so tired of holding on

Letting go was my best decision

I bet you had nights/days

When you were thinking about me

You probably thought that I was going to come back to you

Ha, you probably thought that I wasn't going to leave

I packed up my feelings

I packed my thoughts up

My heart got locked back up from the spare key that you had

Letting go was tough but holding on was even tougher

> "Love from you didn't really show"
>
> —Poetic Tamara

En Route

I'm en route to your heart

Where I plan to be there forever

It might take some time

But trust me

I'm en route to your heart

I'll be there soon

Then we will fall in love

I plan to love you deeply

Antionette Barnes

"I'LL BE THERE SOON"

— Poetic Tamara

THE POET IN YOU, THE POET IN ME, THE POET IN US

*"I'm en route to your heart
Where I plan to be there forever
It might take some time
But trust me"*

En | Route

13
Think back

Think back to all of those times
Where I have been nothing but good to you
And tell me how that made you feel
Because I'm trying to see where I went wrong at

Think back
I'm trying to think back
To all the times you have been good to me
Because there were some good times

I'm trying to think back
To see at what point
You became so distance towards me
It's like the good times are fading aways

"Because I'm trying to see where I went wrong at"

-Poetic Tamara

14 Fading away

The old me is fading away

Only certain pieces will be left behind

Those pieces will be needed to piece

Together the new me

There is love for me out there I know

It will find me soon I hope

Because it feels like this numbness

That I feel with being single is fading away

Antionette Barnes

> "ONLY CERTAIN PIECES WILL BE LEFT BEHIND"
>
> -POETIC TAMARA

15
Just for the record

Just for the record,

        I'm doing great

                In my life

I'm in a great space

        Just for the record,

I've been treating myself better

    Learning myself

        Appreciating myself

Antionette Barnes

"I'm in a great space"

-Poetic Tamara

16. Free time

I wish this is something you'll get

I wish you would squeeze me in more often

However, it's seldom that it happens

Find the time

To have free time

Free time for me

Give me a whole day with you

Make me a top priority

Antionette Barnes

"Give me a whole day with you"

-Poetic Tamara

17

I'm

I'm drifting away
From you
Far away for the time being
Only because

You fell distance from me
I'm going to focus on
Myself more
I have to get myself right

I'm going to be
Thinking of you a lot
I know
This will be a hard thing

> "I have to get myself right"
>
> —Poetic Tamara

Expect

What do you expect from me

To still be the same?

The same old me

That you once had access to?

Do you not expect for me

To grow through life?

You must expect for me

To just go through life?

Well, expect me to

Evolve into the best version of me

Inspire others

Make my dreams come alive

> "Evolve into the best version of me"
>
> —Poetic Tamara

THE POET IN YOU, THE POET IN ME, THE POET IN US

"Do you not expect for me
To grow through life?
You must expect for me
To just go through life?"

Ex | *pect*

Before

Before you got with her,

You was about me

Before she came into the picture,

You used to pop up on me a lot

Before I was really into you,

You used to blow me up a lot

Before you started ignoring me hard,

It was hard for you to keep your hands off me

"You used to blow me up a lot"

-Poetic Tamara

20
Sometimes

Sometimes,

I be wanting a relationship

Sometimes,

I be wanting to remain single

Sometimes,

I be wanting to be in large crowds

Sometimes,

I remind myself that I'm not that type of person

"I be wanting to remain single."
-Poetic Tamara

21 Someone

There's someone for me

I'm sure of it

Well, at times

I don't feel like there is

Is there?

Is there someone for me?

Someone who I can call my own

Because I been having mixed feelings

"Because I been having mixed feelings"

—Poetic Tamara

22 Whole day

I can go a whole day

Not talking to people

Alone

Being at home

I don't mind spending the whole day

Getting myself together

Planning for my future

Being me

"Not talking to people"
-Poetic Tamara

23
Proper care

Handle me with proper care

Show me you truly love me

Appreciate me

Value me

Care for me

With proper care

Listen to me for inner standing

Take caution with me

The old me is what the new me should have been....

"Handle me with proper care"

—Poetic Tamara

THE POET IN YOU, THE POET IN ME, THE POET IN US

"Care for me
With proper care
Listen to me for inner standing
Take caution with me"

Proper | care

 Introducing

Hello, I'm introducing
A more self-aware me
A more loving individual
A confident woman

Pay attention to who I'm introducing
Because this individual communicates their thoughts
This woman is a divine being
She's fascinating

But if that was so, I wouldn't know growth and maturity as I know it today.

> "Pay attention to who I'm introducing"
> —Poetic Tamara

THE POET IN YOU, THE POET IN ME, THE POET IN US

"Hello, I'm introducing
A more self-aware me
A more loving individual
A confident woman"

Intro | ducing

Moments

There are moments

I wish I could get back

Those were great moments

Moments I don't want to fade away

But I know

That I must

Not dwell on the past

I must move forward

There are moments

That I don't want back

Moments that can stay where they're at

Moments that I shouldn't had experienced

Well, I wish that I didn't

Most of those moments

I grew through

Alone

"I grew through"
-Poetic Tamara

The next few pages of this book are cards of different kinds that are meant to be cut out especially the bingo cards games.

Have fun,

Enjoy

Antionette Barnes

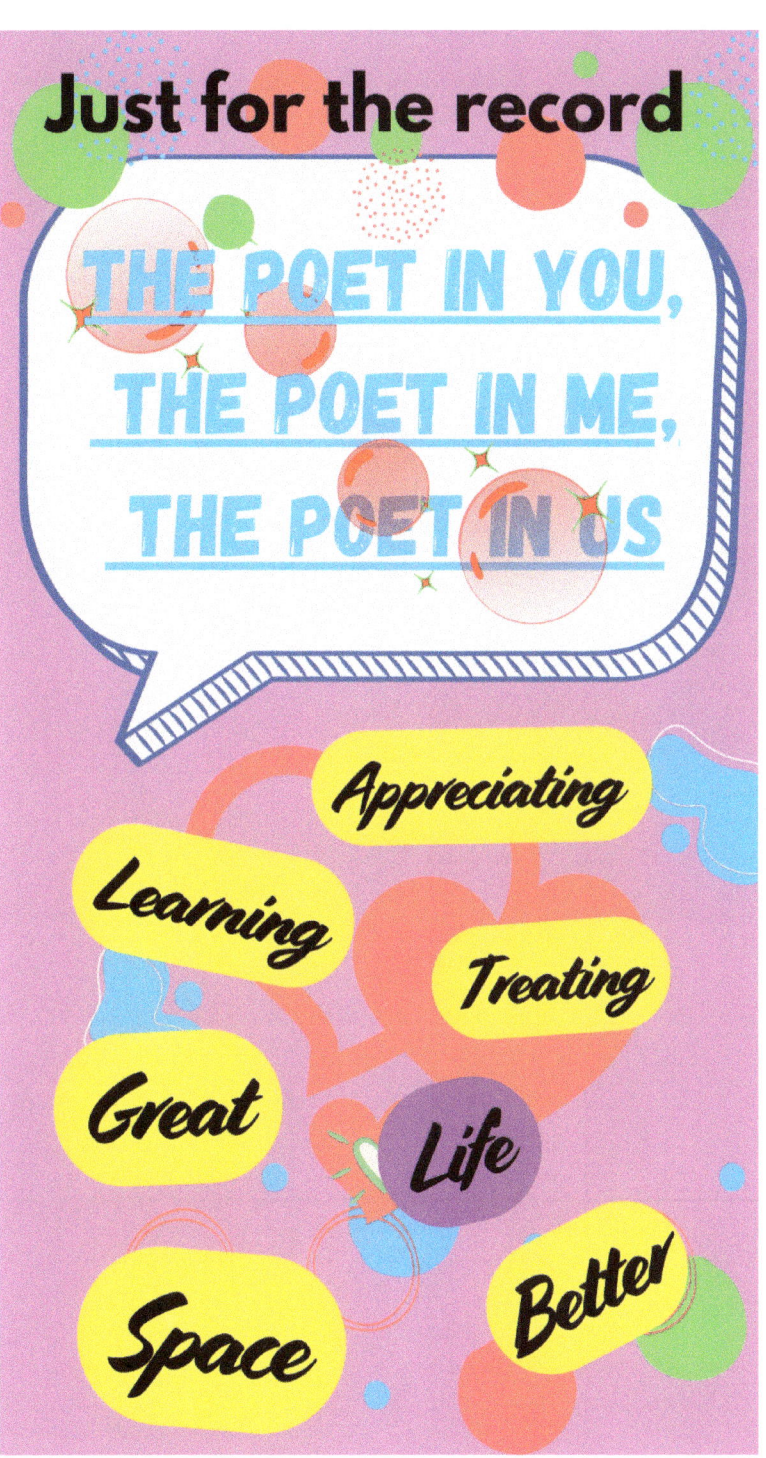

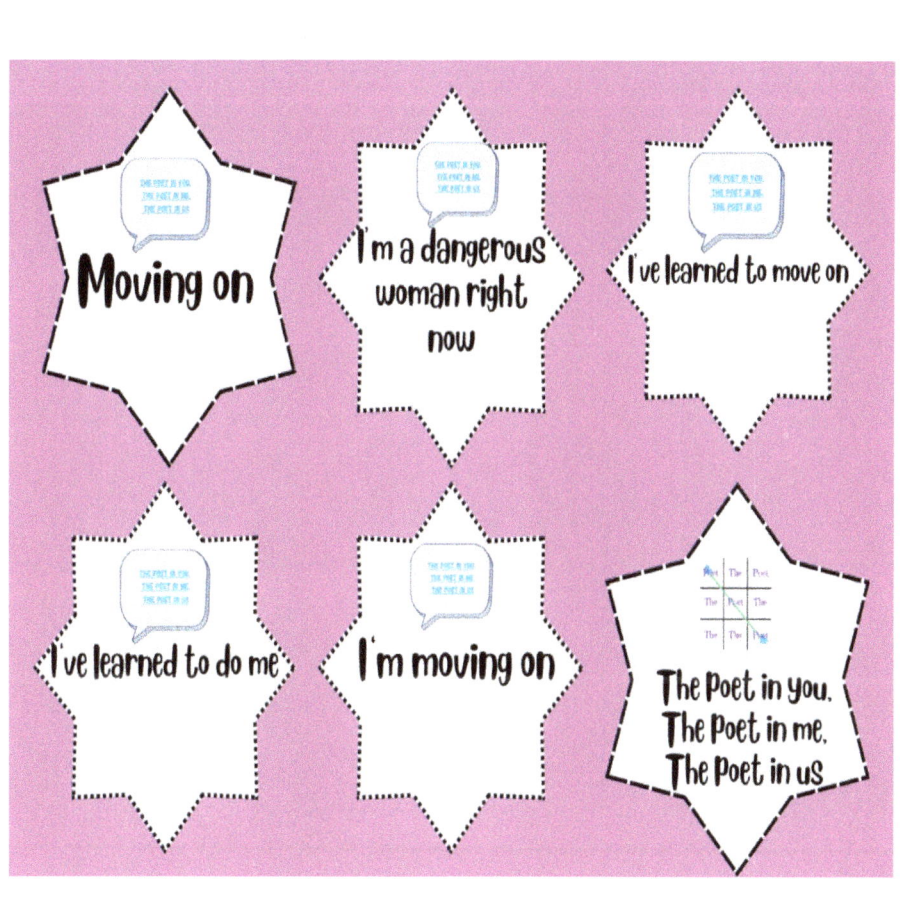

BINGO

THE POET IN YOU, THE POET IN ME, THE POET IN US

Be specific with me	Submissive	Proper care	Inspirations from you
Where do I start?	Letting go	Think back	Before
Whole day	Free space	Introducing	Somehow
Sometimes	Closure	En Route	I'm

BINGO

> THE POET IN YOU,
> THE POET IN ME,
> THE POET IN US

At this point	Moving on	Someone	Proper care
Away from you	Introducing	Moments	Whole day
Just for the record	You left	Free space	Expect
Fading away	Deserve to be happy	Submissive	Free time

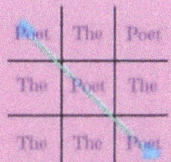

THE POET IN YOU,
THE POET IN ME,
THE POET IN US

Call out card

- AT THIS POINT
- BE SPECIFIC WITH ME
- SOMEHOW
- YOU LEFT
- AWAY FROM YOU
- DESERVE TO BE HAPPY
- MOVING ON
- SUBMISSIVE
- INSPIRATIONS FROM YOU
- WHERE DO I START?
- CLOSURE
- LETTING GO
- EN ROUTE
- THINK BACK
- FADING AWAY
- JUST FOR THE RECORD
- FREE TIME
- I'M
- EXPECT
- BEFORE
- SOMETIMES
- SOMEONE
- WHOLE DAY
- PROPER CARE
- INTRODUCING
- MOMENTS

Other books by Antionette Barnes

- Poetry From The Heart
- Numb to this single life: A collection of poems for all of the single folks
- Leave me to my thoughts
- Going against yourself
- Highly Sensitive People-Don't Forget the Introverts

Journal by Antionette Barnes:

- Unlock What's Deep Inside: An Affirmation Journal

Antionette Barnes

www.ingramcontent.com/pod-product-compliance
Lightning Source LLC
Chambersburg PA
CBHW061739070526
44585CB00024B/2743